SCIENCE STARTERS

On the Move

Wendy Madgwick

RSVP
RAINTREE
STECK-VAUGHN
PUBLISHERS
A Steck-Vaughn Company

Austin, Texas

Titles in this series:
Up in the Air • Water Play • Magnets and Sparks
Super Sound • Super Materials • Light and Dark
Living Things • On the Move

© Copyright 1999, text, Steck-Vaughn Company

Published by Raintree Steck-Vaughn Publishers,
an imprint of Steck-Vaughn Company

Library of Congress Cataloging-in-Publication Data
Madgwick, Wendy.
On the move / Wendy Madgwick.
    p.   cm.—(Science Starters)
    Includes bibliographical references and index.
    Summary: Provides instructions for a variety of
activities which introduce some basic priciples of
physics.
    ISBN 0-8172-5333-5 (hard)
    0-8172-5884-1 (soft)
    1. Force and energy—Experiments—
Juvenile literature.
    1. Motion—Experiments—
Juvenile literature.
    [1. Force and energy—
Experiments. 2. Motion—
Experiments. 3. Experiments.]
    I. Title. II. Series: Madgwick,
Wendy, Science starters.
QC73.4.M33   1999
531'.6'078—dc21
98-30064

Printed in Italy.
Bound in the United States.

1 2 3 4 5 6 7 8 9 0
03 02 01 00 99

Illustrations: Catherine Ward/Simon Girling Associates
Photographer: Andrew Sydenham

Picture Acknowledgments: page 5 The Stock Market/T.
Sanders; pages 10, 12, 16, 18, 26 The Stock Market;
page 11 Trip/H. Rogers; page 23 Bubbles; page 25 Trip/J.
Ringland.

Many thanks to JD, Kaori, Kondwani, Liuzayani, Poppy,
and Shinnosuke.

Words that appear in **bold** in the text are
explained in the glossary on page 30.

Contents

Looking at Movement and Forces

Objects cannot move by themselves. They need a **force** to push or pull them. This book has lots of activities to help you find out about movement and forces.

Here are some simple rules you should follow before doing an activity.

• Always tell an adult what you are doing and ask if you can do the activity.
• Always read through the activity before you start. Collect all the materials you will need and put them on a tray. They are listed on page 28.
• Make sure you have enough space to set up your activity.
• Follow the steps carefully.
• Watch what happens carefully.
• Keep a notebook. Draw pictures or write down what you did and what happened.
• Always clean up when you have finished. Wash your hands.

▶ These skydivers are pulled toward the ground by **gravity**. Find out about this super-strong force on page 6.

Going Down

All objects have a force called gravity around them. This pulls other objects toward them. Big objects have more pulling power than small ones. The earth is so big that its gravity pulls objects down to it.

Fast or slow?

Find a light plastic block and a heavy wooden block of the same size. Put a tray on the floor in front of you. Stand with your arms at the same level. Let go of the objects at the same time. Which one hits the tray first?

Both blocks hit the tray at the same time. Gravity pulls them down to Earth at the same speed.

Thud!

When an object falls, it hits the ground with force. Is the force bigger the farther an object falls? Let's find out.

1 Fill a plastic bowl with wet sand.

2 Hold a marble 10 in. (25 cm) above the bowl. Let it drop into the sand. It will make a hole.

3 Mark the depth of the hole on a strip of cardboard. Measure it. Smooth the sand. Now drop the marble from 20 in. (50 cm), 30 in. (76 cm), and 40 in. (100 cm). Make a chart to show the depth of the hole each time.

The marble makes the deepest hole when it is dropped from 40 in. (100 cm).

Ready, Set, Go!

Objects will not move on their own. You have to apply a force to make them move. You can do this by pulling or pushing an object.

Pulling power

1 Tie a rubber band to an empty toy truck. Put a ruler on the floor beside the truck.

2 Pull the rubber band until the truck starts to move. How far has it stretched?

3 Now fill the truck with toy bricks. Pull the rubber band again.

Did it stretch more or less to make the full truck move?

The rubber band stretched more with the full truck. The farther it stretches, the harder you are pulling it. Heavier objects need more force to start them moving.

Shove off!

1 Rest a cardboard tube against some big books to form a steep slope. Put a toy truck at the end of the tube.

2 Put a ruler beside the truck. Roll a small ball down the tube to hit the truck. Measure how far the truck moves.

3 Fill the truck with toy bricks. Repeat step 2. How far does the truck roll this time? Which truck rolls farther? The empty truck should roll farther.

Let's Slide

Two surfaces rubbing together make a force called **friction**. Smooth things make less friction than rough things.

▲ It is easy to slide down snowy surfaces or over ice. Both surfaces are smooth and make little friction.

Feeling friction
When you rub your hands together, they get warm. This heat is caused by friction.

Super sliders

Let's see what things slide best.

1 Place a wooden block, a small flat rock, an ice cube, and an eraser at one edge of a wooden board.

2 Slowly raise the board until the objects start to slide. Which one starts to slide first? Which ones slide most easily?

The ice cube should move first. The smooth things will move most easily.

Smooth objects move more easily because there is little friction between them and the wood.

◄ We use oil or grease to keep moving parts from rubbing against each other. This reduces friction and helps the parts move more easily.

Slow Down!

Friction tries to keep things from sliding over each other. It slows things down.

▲ This plow has large, knobby tires to grip the slippery, wet soil.

Grip the ground

Try running in slippery socks. Now try it in sneakers. Which is easier? The sneakers help you run. There is friction between the soles of your sneakers and the ground. This helps you grip the ground. It keeps you from slipping when you run.

Getting a grip

2 Tape a sheet of sandpaper over the board. Time the block's slide. Repeat using woolen fabric, foam rubber, and cotton fabric over the board.

1 Rest a smooth wooden board against two large books to make a slope. Put a plastic block at the top. Let it go. Time how long the block takes to reach the bottom.

Make a chart of your results. Which surfaces slow down the block most?

Rough surfaces have the greatest friction. They have the best grip and slow down the brick most.

Rolling Along

Some things are hard to move. Slopes and wheels can make them easier to move.

Super slope

1 Tie a long piece of string to a toy car. Tie the other end to the handle of a toy bucket.

2 Place the car and bucket over a pile of books as shown. Put toy blocks in the bucket. How many blocks are needed to lift the car to the top?

3 Now put a piece of cardboard against the books to make a slope. How many blocks are needed to pull the car up the slope this time? It should take fewer blocks to pull the car up the slope.

Free wheeling

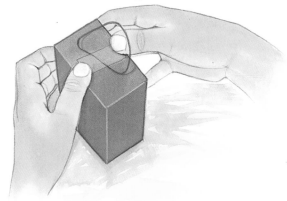

1 Tape a small rubber band to a small cardboard box.

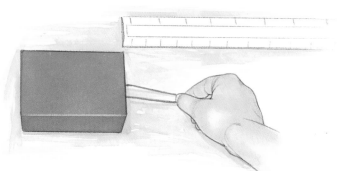

2 Put a ruler on the floor beside the box. Pull the rubber band until the box starts to move. Measure how far the rubber band stretches.

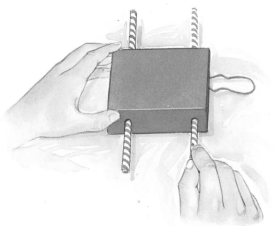

3 Ask an adult to make two holes in opposite sides of the box. Push straws through the holes.

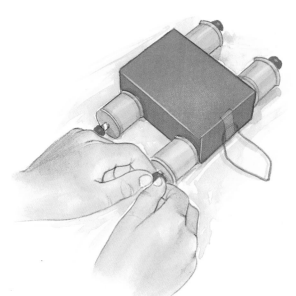

4 Push a spool onto each end of both straws. Attach a ball of modeling clay to all four ends.

5 Move the wheeled box by pulling the rubber band. Does it stretch more or less?

The rubber band should stretch less. It takes less force to move the wheeled box.

Pulley Power

Pulleys are special kinds of wheels.
They help lift heavy loads.

▶ Cranes use pulleys to lift huge loads.

Wind it up

What happens when the girl turns the handle of the truck? The pulley turns and winds up the string. This lifts the load.

Lift a load

1 Tie a string to a toy bucket full of blocks. Tape a stick between two chairs.

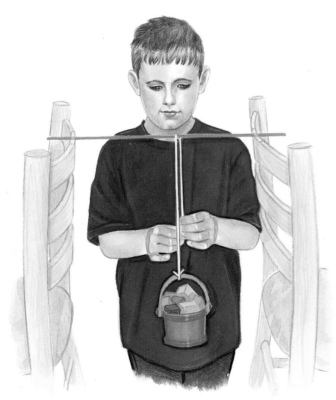

2 Pass the string over the stick. Pull on the string to lift the bucket.

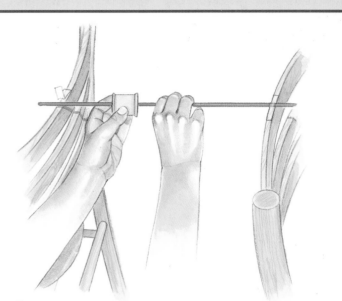

3 Push the stick through an empty spool. Retape it to the chairs.

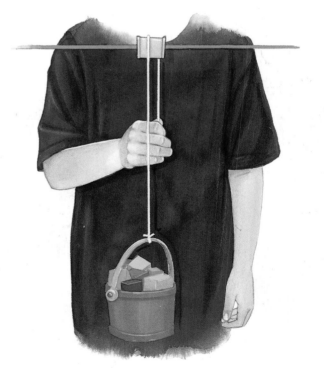

4 Pass the string over the spool and lift the bucket again.

Which bucket is easier to lift? It should be easier to lift the bucket with the spool pulley.

Geared Up

A **gear** is a special kind of toothed wheel. Gears help things turn and move easily.

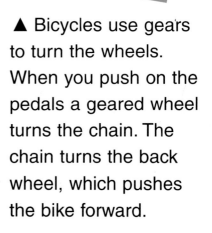

▲ Bicycles use gears to turn the wheels. When you push on the pedals a geared wheel turns the chain. The chain turns the back wheel, which pushes the bike forward.

Beat it

Turn the handle of an eggbeater. Can you see how it turns the toothed wheels? These act as gears to turn the blades of the eggbeater.

Turning power

1 Cut out a large and a small circle of corrugated cardboard. Cut eight toothpicks in half.

2 Push eight toothpick halves into the cardboard evenly around each wheel.

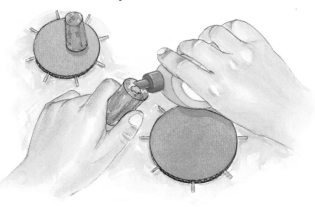

3 Glue a small cork near the edge of each wheel.

4 Push a nail through the middle of each wheel. Push the nails into a thick piece of cork or Styrofoam. Make sure the toothpick "teeth" on the wheels link.

5 Turn the cork handle of one wheel. What happens to the other wheel?

The teeth lock together. They act as gears, which make both wheels turn.

Lifting Loads

A **lever** is a bar that moves on a fixed point. When you push down on one end of a lever, the other end rises. We use levers to help lift heavy things.

Lift it

This can lid is hard to get off. The woman is using a spoon as a lever. She has put one end of the spoon under the lid. She pushes down on the other end. This pushes up the end under the lid. The force of this push lifts off the lid.

Full force

1 Put a wooden bar, about a foot (30 cm) long, across a narrow block of wood. This is your lever.

2 Put a can at one end of the lever. Press down near the middle of the wooden bar. Can you lift the can?

Now press down at the end of the bar. Is the can easier to lift?

The lifting force is bigger the farther away you push from the fixed point. The fixed point of your lever is where the bar rests on the block.

Balancing Points

When things are balanced they do not tip over. They are held in balance by gravity. This balancing point is called the **center of gravity.**

Bend over

Are you good at balancing? Try this.

Put a ball on the floor next to a wall. Stand with your back to the wall. Your heels should be touching the wall. Now try to pick up the ball without moving your feet. What happens?

You can't do it! Your balance point moves forward as you bend over. So you have to move your feet to keep yourself from falling over.

Star acrobat

1 Draw two doll shapes on some thick cardboard (you can trace the ones above). Color one doll as the front and the other as the back. Cut them out.

2 Tape a coin to the inside of each foot.

3 Glue the two halves of the doll together. Let dry.

4 Stretch thick string tight between two chairs. Can you balance the doll on the string?

The weight of the coins keeps the doll's center of gravity in its legs. So the doll should balance.

▲ This girl is doing a handstand. She has to keep her center of gravity over her hands. If she doesn't, she will fall over.

Swinging By

Some machines use swinging movements to make them work. Let's find out about **pendulums**.

Move on

1 Tie a long piece of string between two chairs. Pull it tight.

2 Cut six pieces of string, each one foot (30 cm) long. Tape a marble to each one. Tie the ends of the strings to your string line about an inch (3 cm) apart.

3 Swing one marble to hit the next. What happens to the other marbles?

The first marble hits the second, which hits the third, and so on. The last marble swings out.

Back and forth

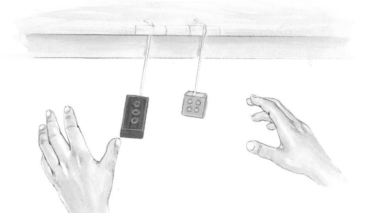

1 Cut two pieces of string, one foot (30 cm) long. Tape a plastic block to one and a smaller block to the other.

2 Tape each string to the edge of a table. Pull the blocks back. Let them go from the same height.

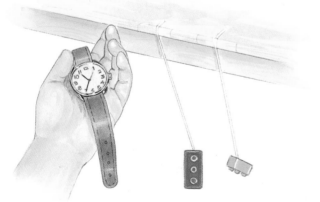

3 Time ten swings for each one. Do they take different times?
The times should be the same for both blocks.

4 Now shorten the strings to 6 in. (15 cm) and time ten swings. Are the times the same as with the long strings? The pendulums with the shorter strings should swing much faster.

▼ Builders use a machine that swings a heavy ball on the end of a chain. This machine can tear down big buildings.

Wind and Water Power

Machines need energy to make them move. Most use gasoline or electricity. Some use the pushing force of water or the wind.

Air power

▲ Wind machines use the pushing force of the wind to make electricity.

1 Make a wheeled boxcar as shown on page 15. Ask an adult to cut out the end and the top of the box.

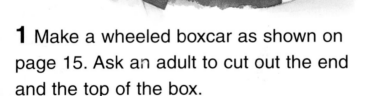

2 Put a balloon into your boxcar. Blow up the balloon. Pinch the end with your thumb and finger to keep the air from leaking out.

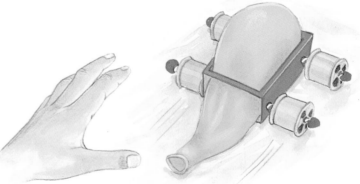

3 Let it go!

The air rushes out of the balloon. The force of the air moving backward pushes the boxcar forward.

Water power

Waterwheels are used to move machinery and make electricity.

2 Push a thin, round stick through the middle of the spool.

1 Collect five small plastic cups. Ask an adult to glue the cups around a spool.

3 Hold the wheel by the stick under gently running water. What happens to the wheel?

The pushing force of the water should turn your wheel.

Materials You Will Need

p. 6 Going Down—a light plastic block and a wooden block of the same size, tray, plastic bowl, wet sand, strip of cardboard, ruler, marble, pencil, and paper.

p.8 Ready, Set, Go!—toy truck, rubber band, ruler, toy blocks, cardboard tube, three or four big books, small ball.

p. 10 Let's Slide—wooden block, ice cube, small flat rock, eraser, wooden board.

p.12 Slow Down!—pair of sneakers, smooth wooden board, two large books, small plastic block, watch with a second hand, sandpaper, woolen fabric, foam rubber, cotton fabric, pencil, and paper.

p. 14 Rolling Along—string, toy car, toy bucket, small blocks, some large books, piece of thick cardboard or board, small rubber band, small cardboard box, ruler, two straws, four empty thread spools, modeling clay. Ask an adult to help.

p. 16 Pulley Power—two chairs, thin stick, tape, toy bucket, small plastic blocks, empty thread spool.

p. 18 Geared Up—eggbeater, corrugated cardboard, round-ended scissors, eight toothpicks, two small corks, glue, two nails, thick piece of cork or Styrofoam. Ask an adult to help.

p. 20 Lifting Loads—board, about 12 in. (30 cm) long, narrow block of wood, small can.

p. 22 Balancing Points—ball, cardboard, colored pencils, round-ended scissors, two coins, tape, glue, thick string, two chairs.

p. 24 Swinging By—string, six marbles, tape, two chairs (you may need two friends to sit on the chairs to keep them still), one large and one small plastic block, watch with a second hand.

p. 26 Wind and Water Power—wheeled box from page 15, long-shaped balloon, five small plastic cups, strong glue, empty thread spool, thin stick. Ask an adult to help.

Hints to Helpers

Pages 6 and 7

Explain that the force of gravity holds most things to the surface of the earth and keeps them from floating in the air. Discuss the fact that you use a lot of energy walking up a steep flight of stairs because you are fighting against the force of gravity.

Explain how Earth's gravity makes falling objects speed up as they fall toward the ground. Their speed does not depend on their weight. The farther the marble falls, the faster it is traveling as it hits the sand. It hits the sand with a greater force and the hole is deeper. Explain that, in order to make the test a fair one, the marble must just be let go, not thrown down. Discuss what would happen to a soft object if it fell from different heights. Suggest that children drop a ball of modeling clay from different heights to see what happens to its shape.

Pages 8 and 9

Discuss the different types of forces, for example, pulling, pushing, and stretching, that the children can use to move an object or change its shape. Talk about whether a small pull or push uses more force than a big pull or push. Explain that the more they stretch a rubber band, the more force they are using. This means that the distance the band has stretched can be used to see how much force is needed to move an object.

Discuss why it is important that, for the test to be fair, the tube must be at the same angle and that the ball should be allowed to roll down the tube, not be pushed. Explain that gravity pulls the ball down the tube. Talk about how the pushing force of the ball as it hits the truck moves the truck forward. The distance the truck moves depends on the pushing force and the truck's weight. The pushing force stays the same, so the loaded truck doesn't move as far as the empty truck.

Pages 10 and 11

Discuss how objects need a force both to start them moving and to stop them from moving. Friction is a force that stops things from moving. In the test, the smooth objects move more easily because there is little friction between them and the wood.

Pages 12 and 13

Discuss how we can use friction to help us move and stop. For example, using the results of the test, discuss how we can increase friction to help us walk on an icy pavement. Talk about the best kinds of shoes to wear for different activities.

Pages 14 and 15

Discuss why it is easier to push or pull things up a gentle slope than up a steep one. Talk about why people use more energy, and get more tired, climbing a steep hill than a gentle one.

Discuss how the wheeled car has less of its surface in contact with the ground than the flat box. Talk about how this will reduce friction and thus help the car move. Discuss how the fact that the wheels turn, rather than drag, along the ground also reduces friction, so that less force is needed to move the car.

Pages 16 and 17

The pulley in the test is a single pulley. It allows you to lift a heavy load directly beneath the pulley more easily. You could try using two spool pulleys (placing the sticks parallel to each other) as a double pulley. A double pulley needs much less pulling force to lift the same load. (Note: a much longer piece of string is needed to raise the load the same distance.)

Pages 18 and 19

Examine how the wheels fit together in an eggbeater. Count how many times the small wheel turns when you turn the big wheel. Each time a larger wheel is turned, it can turn a smaller wheel several times. The number of times the small wheel turns depends on the number of cogs (teeth) each wheel has.

When you turn the big wheel, the teeth should lock and turn the small wheel. The small wheel turns faster. Try adding different numbers of toothpick teeth to each wheel. Try to find out which arrangement turns the small wheel the fastest.

Pages 20 and 21

Explain that using a lever is a simple way to lift heavy loads more easily. Levers increase the pushing force underneath an object, so that a load can be moved with less effort. The farther away the pushing power is from the fulcrum (fixed point), the less force is needed to lift the object. Try putting the can at different distances from the fixed point to see what effect this has on the force needed to lift the can. Levers have a greater lifting power the nearer the object is to the fixed point.

Pages 22 and 23

Discuss how all objects have a point where they are held in balance by the force of gravity. The balance point of a regular shape such as a square is in the center. Explain how objects with a low center of gravity are less likely to topple over. In the doll, the weights in the legs keep the center of gravity low down in the legs, so although more of the figure is above the string, the doll will balance.

Pages 24 and 25

Discuss how a pendulum needs a force to make it start moving. When a swinging pendulum hits another object, the pushing force is passed on. In the first test, the pushing force of the swinging movement is passed on as each marble hits the next one in line. The last marble should swing out as the pushing force of the previous marble hits it. As the last marble swings back, it will send the pushing force back down the line.

Talk about clocks that use pendulums to make them work. Emphasize the two things the tests have shown: the weight on the end of a pendulum does not affect the time the pendulum takes to make one swing; the length of the string does affect the time the pendulum takes to make one swing.

Pages 26 and 27

Discuss the kinds of machines people use to move things more easily. Discuss how machines use energy and forces to make things move. Talk about how a child uses a bicycle to move more quickly. The energy to move the bicycle comes from the child's pushing down on the pedals. This pushing power turns the wheels to move the bicycle. Discuss how natural forces, such as the pushing power of wind and water, can be used to turn wheels and work machines. Talk about why this may be better than using finite fuels such as gas or coal to work machines.

Glossary

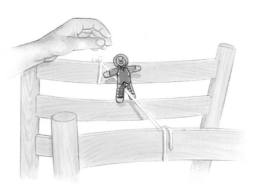

Center of gravity The balance point of an object. When an object is balanced, it does not fall over. An object can balance more easily if it has a balance point near its base, or foot.

Force Something that changes the movement or shape of an object. For example, pushing, pulling, twisting, stretching, and squeezing are all different kinds of forces.

Friction A force that slows down or stops the movement of one surface over another. We use friction to slow things down. For example, brakes use friction to slow down a turning wheel. Friction makes heat and wastes energy. We can reduce friction by putting a layer of oil or grease between moving parts.

Gear A toothed wheel. Two or more gears can connect to help things move. Gears can pass the movement of one set of wheels to another. Gears can be used to move different parts of a machine.

Gravity The force between two objects that pulls them together. It is what pulls all things toward the earth.

Lever A simple machine made up of a bar that moves on a fixed point. Levers can be used to help lift heavy things more easily.

Pendulums Rods or strings that have a weight on one end. They swing back and forth from a fixed point.

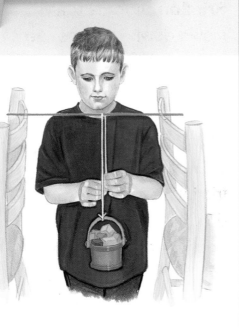

Pulleys Special wheels. A rope fits into a groove around the rim of the wheel. If the end of the rope is tied to a heavy object, the pulley helps you lift the object more easily.

Further reading

Ardley, Neil. *The Science Book of Gravity*. San Diego: Harcourt Brace, 1992.

Dahl, Michael S. *Levers* (Early Reader Simple Science Machines). Danbury, CT: Children's Press, 1998.

——. *Pulleys* (Early Reader Simple Science Machines). Danbury, CT: Children's Press, 1998.

Rowe, Julian. *Make It Move!* (First Science). Danbury, CT: Children's Press, 1993.

White, Larry. *Energy: Simple Experiments for Young Scientists*. Ridgefield, CT: Millbrook Press, 1995.

Index